A Company of Angels

A Company
of Angels

Poems

Florence McNeil

Ekstasis  Editions

Canadian Cataloguing in Publication Data

McNeil, Florence
    A company of angels.

        Poems
        ISBN 1-896860-61-3

            I. Title.
        Ps8525.N43C65   1999   C811'.54   C99-911274-0
        PR9199.3.M4246C65   1999

Cover Art: Hildegaard von Bingen, "*Recycling Lucifer's Fall into Humanity's Glory*," circa 1145.

Published in 1999 by:
Ekstasis Editions Canada Ltd.
Box 8474, Main Postal Outlet
Victoria, B.C. V8W 3S1

Ekstasis Editions
Box 571
Banff, Alberta ToL oCo

THE CANADA COUNCIL | LE CONSEIL DES ARTS
FOR THE ARTS | DU CANADA
SINCE 1957 | DEPUIS 1957

A Company of Angels has been published with the assistance of a grant from the Canada Council and the Cultural Services Branch of British

Contents

Part 1: A Company of Angels: Dream   7

Dream: A Company of Angels   9
Rock Life   11
Thanksgiving   13
An Announcement   14
A Funeral In Late Summer   16
Season Of Rest   18
Birth   19
Hospital Exit   20
My Father's Presents   21
War   23
On The Scottish Island: The Commitee To Bring In The Bull   25
The Silver Nuns   27
Inlet People   28
Accommodating Spring   30

Part 2: A Company Of Angels: Lewis Carroll   37

Prologue   39
Professor Dodgson, cleric, mathematician, storyteller   40
1898 (1)   41
"There are questions I visualize"   42
Charles Dodgson's Mother   43
The Fireplace   44
River Bank Thoughts   45
"I have loved the stage"   48
An old bachelor   49
Miss Prickett   50
The Mirror Image   51
The Credo of the Looking Glass People   52
Alice Liddell   53
"In the darkroom, Alice"   55

Alice meeting the fawn   56
The Red Queen and the White Queen: Lewis Carroll on Women 57
       The Red Queen   57
       The White Queen   58
Mrs. Liddell   59
Shakespeare for young girls   60
Dreaming   61
Alice on the Stage   62
"In the looking glass"   63
Charles Dodgson, photographer   64
A Theology Lecture   65
Irene Barnes, a young friend   66
1898 (2)   67
Epilogue: Alice in New York, 1932   68

Part 1:

A Company of Angels:
Dream

Dream: A Company of Angels

There are troops plodding in some war
my father is with them
I do not know this war
with its ancient and submissive rage
its theories of balloons or airships
or generals in glass cages
or landing craft that hold the soldiers still
so their pictures can be taken in blood
What years separate the line to death
the quick embracing of a family
who will identify them and move on
their feet marching in place
like the rotations
of tractors

And yet awake I know
my father never went to war
he was no explorer of machine guns
or bayonets
he saw the air somersault with fire
only at a distance

His war was private
the long infliction of the sea
the blatant word: home
scrubbed out of his vocabulary
lined up with the others
at the rail   the docks
his eyes flecked with sun and wind
the doors that closed and opened,
the shining rocks
the numbing chores
the ship circulating   the words
coming back but always there
unchanged
my father at the rails hoping
(as the soldiers)
with exultation and despair
for the deliverance of the storm.

Rock Life

I

The snakes have come to our shore
I watch them half out of the rocks
baking their scales
in the sunlight

I think sometimes they have more choice than we

having known
nothing beforehand they
die preserved
in iridescence
under wheels

or in the pink fingers
of little boys
who covet rainbows

Our enemies are known
and waited for
we plan them into our
course of living
they are convenient
and always ready

and so living conveniently
we die the same
stretching ourselves out finally
on colourless skin
reflecting more ice that sun.

II

Designed for rocks
the barnacles
extend their filaments
in time
a concert
of slender saxophones
soundless
their tides
regulated by
a larger rhythm

I sense these
minuscule
musicians
are defensive
when I near

I step around them
conscious of
some primitive
responsibility

trespassing
in the energetic limbo
that grips the sand
between earth
and ocean.

Thanksgiving

We were struggling against the wind
on the street glazed with sunlit shoppers
and she came upon us
we had left the glass restaurant
sated with quiche and latte
I had turned to you, there was a hand
and someone I remember only as a smudge
of brown in the glare, hair blowing in severed strands
over her face,
the hand, a voice asking quietly for money
I felt in my pocket, murmuring I was sorry
what was I sorry for that her stick figure
briefly static, medieval
had intruded on safe ground
it was momentary, like a flash in a newsreel
a face of many faces lined up in wars
or collections
and yet as unexpected as a close up
of an execution
she was not young
we met at the splayed edge of the sidewalk

So they have moved uptown now
among the boutiques they live, or sing
or hold out their eyes to you

I cannot bear it
It will be thanksgiving, I will concentrate
on our table

I will shut out till night
the linear persistence of that figure
and my part in its creation.

An Announcement

No one should die over the phone
yes says the voice   she's gone
words jump up and down
along the racing wire
I watch humming birds
leaping in anger
over the feeder
tiny and fervent their wings strip the air
like flies caught on paper
a child chases another child
on a gleaming cycle
there is news of rebels in
some country taking over
a holiday inn
I can picture the hotel
because I know where the round desk
carpet   manager are placed
all over the world
It is the rebels I cannot see
Or you   without life
without the endearing perversity
of your grin
the comic turns you remembered from
our childhood
when we starred in colourful scenarios
chasing backwards and forwards
collapsing into laughter
I remember   the telephone says
what fun she was

we are smiling at each other now
back in some lost time
the afternoon turns black and silver
our madcap race   the tumult that we shared
reduced to voices
private
unravelling.

A Funeral In Late Summer

It was at first a ceremonial occasion
meaning we were meeting with nods and smiles
children who have
cultivated wrinkles
whose pictures have changed
like watercolours caught in a cold rain

only our eyes are signalling

until the coffin blocks our reminiscing

I am holding the memorial card
I am trying to concentrate on the
wreaths that stand
where the communion rail
used to be

you were there   you held out your hand
but it is your child who looks at me
with your startling face

there was music in another August
we stood behind the closed door
trying to pretend
we understood the dance

I would never have opened the door without you
I would have liked you to know that   my lost friend

but there is other music now
the wheels of the coffin
passing relentlessly down the aisle

and the priest who never knew you
is pouring out libations
singing among the darkened relatives
his long inevitable lamentation.

Season Of Rest

The flowers of autumn are
ranged today
deep subordinate colours
flanking the wooden fence
I have accumulated myself
through all these seasons

What do you notice

a heron wraps itself around the sky
fish leap out of the slanted ocean
and I am here
attached to this yard
unable to move up
past the cylindrical clouds
or out: fence upon fence
makes its own statement

winter can only be liberating

when the door closes
on all these expansions
my face might
show up for you
in the shortened ceremonies
of water and light
when the fire newly lit
throws its insinuations
into obscure corners.

Birth

The safety of the spring blossoms
you, covered, sealed,
your face taken from hers
reflecting something so new
there is no name for it yet

not knowing what the day will hold

and the woman—if she could
would keep you fastened to her
wet and clawing
unable to take your picture
out of her silver frame

it is as well
that she become preoccupied
with her own image
in her own unwinding
cannot follow you

splayed against the sky
with the eagle hovering
restlessly behind a cloud.

Hospital Exit

Throw open the door!
Let out the inmate!
There will be no recovery in this sanitary dusk
flattening
the beds
stains upon the glass
the air fluid with infections
coupling the light
like summer spots
you are a sheet a number
a hand tolls your biography
you are sinking in centimetres

If they wheel you to the door
you will find feet, grass, an
abundance of actors
the world growing and spilling
without the travail of your locked room
voices white and electric
among them, yours, now recognizable
leaving the period of moans
the starch, modulation,
the full stop.

My Father's Presents

My father lived to give away
no family treasure
was safe from his
overweening generosity
he handed out Christmas presents
(his own and the family's)
with the same enthusiasm
with which he proffered
puppies and kittens
that arrived in predictable
quantities
several times a year
In between jobs he made
toys
wooden artifacts imaginative
and inaccurate
their defects the result of
his impatience
and the derelict ocean lumber he collected
No one visited without a trophy
sometimes hidden from my mother
who watched over the
diminishing cupboard supplies
with alarm

I remember our last Christmas
together
when old and sick
he slumped unhappily in
the frontroom chair
staring at the ocean, the bursting forest
until his eyes caught fire
"You'll need a Christmas tree" he said
and made plans for the chase and capture
of the largest one we ever had
after he rested   for a while
And so we held him as he climbed the hall
steering him slowly towards the steep bed

That day and the next we waited
knowing the children would arrive
and yet reluctant to buy a tree
wrapping the hordes of Christmas gifts
that seemed to have no destination.

War

I
End of the Century

Now this ocean across my face (this ocean, not the one that
faces you wherever you are, your view uncluttered by death,
by the lurch of a tree across your horizon). Can we speak
easter in this spring filled with forgotten crystal, stars
that shout poison out of the sky, hungry faces tunnelled towards
the lightning blurring the screen, as the forsythia,
the plum blur what we are coming out of: the dim wail of the lines
which travel vertically body after body towards nothing
we are capable of comprehending, this jaded shame, that we
have thrown away the century and yet the mutilated children
still linger in their frozen shapes.

II

Waking at night
the scimitars of trees
decapitate the sky
I know there is still a war on my radio
and it will be recounting itself in breath, whispers.
testaments reversing themselves

I should bring an orderly process
into my nightmares

but someone is playing his computer
and others are being spilled

fear eats me like a hyena severing the plains

if I light up the night
my room might be next

in the morning the computer is still at work
its deadly hum cornering all the stations
all the channels

it will come to me in print

the final decision: to set it all down
to authenticate
the tidy tribes of the late century
at their sacrileges.

On The Scottish Island:
The Commitee To Bring In The Bull

The Island's leading gentlemen in their white hair
and only ties
puff their pipes importantly
hold their caps like generals
before a certain victory
they are not often called upon
to make a decision
as monumental as this
bringing in the Spring Bull
who will litter the Island
with his descendants
(in a land where heredity is important)
the stones are mossy
the periwinkles   primroses
sway through the rain
the heather crawls with new growth
the Fishing Fleet gnaws at its moorings
Somewhere in Paris or London
or New York
there may be more important decisions
where stockbrokers may throw statistics
in each others eyes
To these men awaiting their celebrity
their voices urgent with Spring
there is nothing more insistent
life on the Island depending on the lambs the fish
and the fiery organs
of the minotaur

they will raise up
who will gather around him admiring throngs
and the velvet hills will dance with calves and milk
the bull   sire   hero   dairyman
will retire   crowned with Gaelic adulation
to his own Elysian fields
having signed for the grateful Islanders
an album of his personal reproductions.

The Silver Nuns

The silver nuns shine like bells
in the supermarket
two by two   they are dancing past
the alluring shelves
where objects are hung with signs that say
buy me
or eat me
The silver nuns freed from their
long skirts and capes
from the bonnets that enclosed them so they saw
only ahead like obedient horses
are ringing with carefree excitement
as they skate with their new legs
to the tinned choir
their tinselled hair permed
their mouths dotted with insinuations of lipstick
the silver nuns forever on vacation
offer their glittering new hands
to the crowds
who see them now only through their merriment.

Inlet People

They lived at the base of a steep hill below our house   disconnected
from our neighbourhood belonging neither to sea or land holding
on like lichen to the shore   they appeared in the lean years of boxcars
and battered heads   when the thin families nailed together their walls
nailing them in square patterns   cereal boxes on sticks   which
stretched in a rigid looping to end in the spattered sky of the oil
refinery   they stayed when there seemed no need   officially untaxed
unnoticed   when the war erupted like mushrooms on all sides of
them and jobs were plentiful   and even after when the cloud
dispersed   becoming fanciful now their square houses growing turrets
drawbridges windmills flags flying beside the lacy curtains and the
houses now trimmed in blood red ochre yellow splashed alongside
the tracks   the trains spitting silt over their landscape and women
cleaning cleaning fighting the tides the steam the barrier of the great
hill   and now they walked more proudly women with ravaged faces
softening   their eyes unveiling   men with wounded hands carrying
lumber tools moving backwards and forwards   and children in
groups held together as they ascended   they were knocking on doors
in the forbidden neighbourhoods and screens were wedged open
until the hostile faces melted into dialogue   as they stood on
doorsteps smelling of low tide and lumber of pie baking and soft
mould of leather footballs and herded clothes   and their houses grew
dining rooms   glass ornaments that struck light on the window sills

and so we visited the Inlet people in summer carrying our bathing
suits invading their territory   changing behind the spare bushes
rocked by trains   moving sharply into the cold green water where logs
seagulls wrappers excrement floated by   the Inlet people peering from
their balconies waving at us offering us lemonade   their small babies
rounding in the sun   officially unnoticed and free to enlarge on their
gifts to children who came down their hill   they are in my memory
lined up by their houses women in print dresses whose flowers
echoed the boxes of sweetpeas men now gardening in terraces

competing with the wind and tides and children briefly come from their tethered boats built by their fathers or uncles they have stopped now for my picture   staring out in their plenitude (I have glossed over the grey shacks   the crippled faces)   they look up at me and smile in hopeful innocence not seeing the tidal wave that is to come officially noticed   they are deemed real people in real houses and as such are dispensable the houses woven slowly through the years are unravelled in a morning and there are broken threads fires and floating sticks and the Inlet people standing in the smoke without their walls on the curled linoleum floors sorting through the pieces

I have no snapshot in my mind of the cleared shore returned almost to the sea.

Accommodating Spring

i

Something is dragging itself across my horizon
in segments
it is a time to announce death
the relatives are being removed one by one
the pink symbols of the new sky
the pieces of camellia, currant,
are bouquets at a funeral home

I have always welcomed the parade of April
now it is one more month to die
to count the time rope by rope
bead by bead
toward a parting of the curtain

There was always a new pair of birds
before
a new link in a circular chain
fragile and breathtaking as a daisy wheel
meaning you counted and came back

Now it is frayed
or the tinsnips have done their duty

It is hard to think of spring
as already dismembered.

ii

It's April
the trees are breathing now
the kittens leaping in the first bite of sun
the tall lines of birds
clamouring for leaves

the grass making tunnels in the morning

the dying cat sits on the
lawnchair
(leftover from September)
her coat bred into titian beauty
still floats around her
Breath moves the bloated flanks
in and out in and out

I pick her up
feeling the bones   the paper skin

the light catches her golden eyes

I look at her through tears

I want it all to stop
her beauty
the unmerciful splendour of spring.

iii

I am not sanguine about our chances
yet what to do
with all these flowers making prints
in the grass
the move from dark to light
when even the black elements
a young eagle   a hawk
a far away boat in a shadow
have beauty
spring should be no more   this year
than a centre light
switched on
while the nightmares continue
nowhere to clear the eyes
and yet it carries seeds and sun
across a long blue sky
and a certain timbre
in the speculation of birds.

iv

A large cat head
an orange moon
over the flip side of the sky
you have brought home
arrangements of pussy willows
embryonic bubbles
caught in their opening chorus
what they might have gone on to
is redundant
march will not fire them off
in harmony with frog sounds
or fern births

the farmers will not aim their bird guns
into their branches

they will never open their sheets
to transient green wings

from the moving turntable then
one perfect note: the silver buds
set delicately upon their never being.

v

The boy in the clown pants
is at the door
spring patches: squares, triangles
frog shapes
(behind him leaden skies
they are deceptive
scratch and you will find blue
voluptuous resonant
I believe that now)
the morning has been filled with asides
an old diary cracked like seaweed
someones's birthday to overcome
relatives whose impromptu polaroids
are tin now
khaki coloured
in their mechanical trenches
I am tired of liberating them
they are being drawn like myopic lily pads
into the full sun.
The boy at the door
bringing april
wants nothing in return
not the ceasefire from my crisp relatives
or my thanksgivings.

vi

I have put on a new skin for tulip viewing
Stepping into fresh grass, hailstones of blossoms,
The sky shedding clouds over an uncreated tree
ready like the month to stretch up and up
breaking through in volcanic new perceptions
I too am shedding indoor beliefs that
do not hold up to the rigours of warmth
every winter I am finished, all is clear,
the text printed, immutable
yet every spring it is the same
there is no answer, no elucidation,
all questioning, journeying,
demanding revision,
perhaps only abandonment.

vii

I examine the minutiae of rain
how it beads in numerical order
like a sheer abacus
so one can see in April
beyond the counting
the feathers on trees
the faces that perch on windows
to waver   /spring
ratcheting the faces
higher and higher   /spring
I can spell it back now
The graves we stood over
that other rain
that slanted over the terrible wreaths
the livid unnatural roses
already buried
If I can see at night still
in the penetration of shadows
those people I loved and sent away
who might be waiting for me
How surprising then
after I have closed the wet gates
of the cemetery
and accept
that the new sun
rimming the daffodils
has a tentative warmth
that the sequined puddles are sinking slowly
drying out.

Part 2:

A Company Of Angels:
Lewis Carroll

Prologue

Unleashing parades of interpreters who would
peer into the rabbit hole
with cynical delight
signifying a new century
where eccentricity became
an inappropriate word
something to tuck away with the lacy valentines
the hoop skirts
the small groupings of
parents and children
who sat rigidly around an over–elaborate table
and played their games

Now that we know everything
have regimented all the pawns
and sent the white knight charging on his horse
into a doomed world
bloated with our own vocabulary
we have no synonym
for wonderland

Professor Dodgson, cleric, mathematician, storyteller:

numbers whirling to infinity
the sea spinning the sky
testing the corners
of the universe
through an everlasting
tunnel
fraught with
universal prohibition
at the corner of the stars
one sad white knight
gently
kneeling
on uneven ground.

"My life has been so strangely free from all toil and trouble, that I cannot doubt my own happiness. . ."

1898 (1):

Looking back on it all,
I could say it has been happy,
though the child, of quite unearthly beauty, was only
glimpsed once,
in a London exhibition, face to face, and only briefly,
and I have ever since never ceased to look for her,
wanting to capture, silently, within the boundaries of my camera
the perfect innocence unadorned, the thought of the small body,
white as sunlight on a bell tower,
she was never there, in the railway carriages, at the public beaches
she retires behind an open book, is covered by the bathing tent
with its large jaw taking in the burdened child and
spitting her out in lingering silk that parts among the waves,
I have carried my bag of tricks, games, safety pins to
hold up the skirts of tiny waders,
and have fended off boys,
who even in the most polite and mannerly
have the tendency to turn quite easily into animals,
need always to be covered.

There are questions I visualize when I
lie
prone upon an ancient meadow
where buttercups rush in a summer wind
there are pieces of sky above me
and faces with smiles, ears and
eyes, omnipotent faces
(the creator's art writ large on the
sistine walls)
but always disembodied
That this is so
disturbs me
but the head containing all wisdom
floats and fades among the
white and blue clouds
appears on branches
is there beside the first star

I sometimes think: to have the body
is to court decapitation
to hear crowds of wavering cards
screaming for your demise
to be admonished,   or flogged,
or shrunk by an accumulation of years

I am a child again,
I am beside my father and there is something
on the edge of my tongue,
he turns, and in dark syllables, says to me:
Do Not Ask.

Charles Dodgson's Mother:

My father's picture still frowns at me,
and so I concentrate upon my mother,
gentle, fixed in her portrait with a
circular frame of tangled leaves,
I see her still, and yet she was always in motion,
spreading love to the babies who came one after another,
and displaced me,
so on the mount there was always one being held,
while I lurked in the corner and prepared
games and puzzles for anyone's delight
In my parents' bedroom dark curtains were a shield
and what cries came out of that room
I closed my mind against,
told by a friend of babies coming, of their slippery arrival,
not with clouds of glory, but with blood and membrane
decorating their nakedness
I boxed his ears and closed my own
and climbed my mother's breast
and leaned against the embroidered gown,
my mother, washed and pristine,
so beautiful, her face a magic lantern through which
I witness the world.

Her leaving when I was nineteen, her leaving before
my camera could connect with her,
has set my memories on fire.

The Fireplace

Life has descended to me through the fireplace
the hearth   its tiles radiating
comforting positions
I am alone
my mother leaves the others
offers me unstinted admiration
(love is too strong a word
belongs to the indignities of lower orders
who live in one room
without a fireplace
and radiate towards each other)
the fire ignited sends
warmth into my characters
they arise from their cardboard preoccupations
to waltz around the flower strewn room
are dark in the corners
light as they draw closer
illuminated now
so I can press them in my book
their colours enhanced even further
in my preservation.

River Bank Thoughts

i

The dragonfly folds on my finger
dropping its ragged sails
written on
by the cat
The air is full of
the tolling of gnats
that rings out August's perfection
There should be no deaths
by the river
not here where hostilities have ceased
and a wicker cloud
slides over the sun.

ii

I am not willing to concede
that the sky will stay
powdered with
winter I believe it will draw open
and float down upon
a stream
assembling
the startling
anagrams of summer.

iii

I drew my tales
with butterfly antennae
the round fans of
daisies
the August Alice world
before the tales
tumbled away from me
dropping down down
into the validity of my past
or the traces of altered dreams.

I have loved the stage
as a child became conjuror
the most amazing trick
was the rapidity with which
I stretched out
moved from boy to man
while my imagination
refused all suggestions
I entertained the family
with puppets
tiny figures who burst
through the scenery
their voices falling in
the slanted afternoon
(they were impudent   said no to my father
rang up their own curtains)
I continued dispatching
my little skits
long into the evening
arranging my childhood
as I saw fit
bringing in new puppets
who sat for me on the river bank
while they spoke my stories
They have not been a complete success
turning intractable
breaking their strings
refusing to duplicate
my catechism.

An old bachelor:

I have set my life by my pocket watch
and am never late
walk gently through my rounds
exactly at the appointed hour
numbering in various languages
the hours
my book of days starting
with my soul rung out in chapel
ending late, late, while I am still listing
pictures, notes, diaries, letters,
books, my sins,
I walk like a military person,
marshalling my facts, inspecting them in
lines which never tire me,
I use cardboard place mats,
my lunch is bread and wine
I extend myself always with my top hat
feel neither hot nor cold, and
thus dispense with extra clothes.

go nowhere if I am invited

allow myself only along the
edges of the manuscript
the small infractions
of scrolls and feathers

Miss Prickett:

The governess to the Liddell children
construes my constant visits as
perhaps more than is meant
or less
she is not highly educated her mind
could not fathom the depth of
my boating with the little girls
my pictures, the children, Alice
settling herself onto the glass plates,
my carpet bag which open reveals snap dragons,
wire contortionists,
to hear the laughter of Alice,
I am as blissful as a bridegroom
(a figure of speech, you understand,)
need no relations with Miss Prickett, in her
dark gown, patterned on the bare trees,
stripped to its sobriety,
set against the fluid springtime of
my Alice.

The Mirror Image

Mr. Carroll was slightly askew
(as was Mr. Dodgson)
a smile that tilts on one side,
opening slowly to a serious conclusion,
their eyes were sea blue
the blue of an ocean
filled with small waders on
an affecting day
the day of a white stone
and yet if one moves closer to the glass
one notes the unevenness, the level
not exact,
one shoulder carried higher than the other in
a half shrug,
as if dismissing increased fame,
they remained mirror thin,
and walked, though upright
in a jerky fashion
as though they were a knight in armour
destined forever to be off their horse

they were always content with their own inventions

The Credo of the Looking Glass People

If you desire to walk with us
you must see it is along straight lines
you must not detour to smile upon trees
with crooked branches
or admire the deviance of pawns wriggling along the squares
you must take life so literally
that it makes nonsense
of language
seeing the garden much better from the hill
in its midst there are only assorted pawns
some fallen
language with no ornament
with a meaning that is one–dimensional
and only what we wish to give it

Carry no allusions

These are our stated aims

We must not wander   Alice
must not look at the underside of meanings
the gamut of possibilities.

Alice Liddell:

Alice with her tiny face, her hair short,
cut like a knight's page,
my special friend,
boating with me on the Thames,
her sisters their eyes caught in an afternoon flame,
laughed like flowers all afternoon,
but Alice fastened upon my brain
and impelled a story,
so now looking back on that golden afternoon,
the fourth of July
the water lilies rowing by,
the oars spilling like lemonade into the river,
the words sound over and over to me
like a gramophone,
the horn blaring in a quiet voice,
my voice, the cylinder stuttering, until finally
the words are ripe and fall into
a book.

Alice I caught with my camera alone,
her form so light she might have floated off,
and needed to be anchored in my memory
or attached to the sisters on whom she leaned as if
they were turkish pillows
almost the perfect child, the one whose face rose from the crowd,
and challenged me,
almost, but not quite.

Alice I took at thirteen, catching her on
a satin chair
her hands held sadly
as if they were not her own,
her hair poured, distended, her dark eyes
now pooled with shadows,
and under the rosebud bodice, the
small, intrusive bumps showing too clearly

her voice did not call to me

Alice dismissed into another world

And now the records indicate that July the fourth
of 1862
was wet and cold.

In the darkroom, Alice, her face solemn
as a rabbit, but not frightened,
posed, the liquid slowly revealing
tantalizing eyes, she is beside me,
her laugh winding its way off into the
deepest, lost woods
where branches of cheshire cats sing to her
she is before me, Alice mirrored,
Alice entranced with her spreading self
calling to her sisters to see the evidence
At this point precisely I turn her over to
Tenniel
who protests her dark beauty, small significant
expressions
and creates hair that is long and fair
streaming on her shoulders in varying bursts
has her innocent, and vacant,
carrying in her arms a squirming pig.

Alice meeting the fawn:

Such a lovely creature its body
soft and yet rigid, stopping for me
to place my hands about its neck
to kiss its head which feels both rough and tender
as the wind unsettling the ocean
on a summer day
I shall proceed with it lovingly
towards the next square
where the crown
awaits
adding to my body
a certain height and distinction

And yet the fawn and I cannot exchange names
neither of us remembering who we are
and being unnamed must remain
creatures in a dream
advancing through an obscure wood.

The Red Queen and the White Queen:
Lewis Carroll on Women

The Red Queen:

What do I represent to you
running along in my boxes
among the squared off trees
I am old   I have Alice by the hand
I am a model of rectitude
I would stand with my arms akimbo
if you had not made them so immovable
I can move them only in mannequin poses
Where do I fit in your world
seen dimly
through a mirror lit by a chandelier
where the jets sputter and go out
loping across the board like an
obsessed pony
going nowhere
I am a girl grown up   I have warts on my wooden chin
am governess   nag   a portrait of Victoria
frowning upon her subjects
Receding in my smoky glass
You can never believe in me
So you have put a crown on my head
and bound me to a book.

The White Queen:

You have seen me "gentle, stupid, fat and pale,"
a woman whose hair escapes the fluted crown
and tumbles about her face
whose wit is woolly
I do not know how to love Alice
though I am kind to her in the way
a large pink sow is well disposed to
her piglets
I cannot keep two thoughts in my
circular head
and so I bestow them upon
the red queen   my running mate
who being forceful
a fury who exacts from the universe
specific manners
can keep her own thoughts,
my watery considerations,
and even the tainted curiosities
of Alice.

Mrs. Liddell:

The fine weather saw Mr. Dodgson
cluttering up the edges of our yard
his camera waiting, lurking,
like a startled hare in the shrubbery
wanting always to see my daughters
with the insistent
enormous eye of the camera
so I come across them, grouped, their dark heads blending
in a trio
unsmiling, frozen in the warm sun,
Alice he especially courts
she has moved from his picture to his stories
and in doing so
has removed herself too far from mine.

Shakespeare for young girls:

That no licentious word should reach those ears—
so pink, curled like cushioned sea shells—
enter their delicate souls,
I am revising a revision of Shakespeare.
Reading through the altered text, I find
too much has been left
words that might shame the alabaster cheeks of
small maidens
I am set upon this task
slimming the bard to acceptable speech
arranging words, so I might add them to
my black bag
among the small complicated treasures
I have invented

Dreaming:

I know when I dream I create or move into
a world that is perfectly formed and understood
and I know precisely why I have to fall
and what phantasm rushes after me
in circling darkness
and why it must appear again
enclosing me   shutting me out of the garden
where flowers spin towards each other
or singly divest themselves of enclosing leaves
their faces illuminated
in the sun
I cannot reach   the door remaining always
in the comfortable shade

Alice on the Stage:

Here are my notes:
Do not let Alice be other than a fawn
pure, gentle, her figure so courteous
she might fly off at any moment,
the White Rabbit should have spectacles
the Queens should have dignity
amid the rotating landscape
But you see, you could never get it right —
I sent Alice down the rabbit hole
with no notion of what she knew
there is nothing substantial
my story belongs to dragonflies
weaving their curious webs on the
August river
or the leaves that crashed to the ground
in October
as porous and repetitive as the
sound of the Oxford bells
tolling Alice's inevitable age.

In the looking glass
I see myself
framed   I am peering
through the camera eye
which can only go backwards
the face I surrender to the plates
is not the one I have now
but which I had minutes ago
I am ranging indelicately
between very old
and very young
there are a series of mirrors
set up like stations
but I know longer know
which direction is
amenable
the formula is set
the brief pause
to validate the journey
fixing time, date, mouth and eye positions
the smile, the waistcoat
stiffened upon the chair
the clamp securing the frozen nick
When it is taken   the subject
—myself—
released
closer to death.

Charles Dodgson, photographer:

The children should be posed in simple nightgowns,
flannel—having more texture and colour than cotton—
their tiny bodies dispensed from the
hoops and starches, the laced up rigidity,
which holds them upright so their movements become static,
walking, even running, a series of stiff portraits,
little girls, soft as spun wool or the down that floats
from greeting cards
ought never to be encumbered,
and so emancipated might refrain from growing.

Could I, in all purity, picture them naked,
I should do so,
and in fact have won the grudging yes of mothers—
to take girls, radiant in their white bodies,
those who do not have a modest shrinking
from such exposure,
but shine like haloes in my wooden backdrop.

Boys, however, always need clothes.

When I am gone (as I see the end come closer),
I have insisted these portraits
be destroyed,
wishing to save the girls,
who will grow taller, larger,
fill out the screen with dimensions I do not care for,
wishing to save their dignity,
and yet my heart aches at the thought of the paper children
burning, their edges wisped, curled up, becoming,
ashes.

A Theology Lecture

Only children are able to absorb
strange things and let them
be strange
I am attempting to converse
with grown up people
who are listening for the moral
they rustle   their bones creak
upon their frames
they watch my stuttering mouth
in some bewilderment
my fictions have not added to their incomes
their upright perceptions of themselves
If there is laughter in paradise
I have not reached the holy land
in this company
their faces turn to each other
they are saying
who is this implacable person
I am explaining something serious:
the innocent garden
before the fall: I am the Reverend Mr. Dodgson
but out of my mouth the jabberwock slips
one of God's jests
escapes to the night sky.

Irene Barnes, a young friend:

I remember Mr. Dodgson, remember his face,
young and fresh as though he had stepped new born into
a world I could not follow
his hair was white, and tousled, a head of sails,
as if he might move off gently in a favouring breeze,
around children, he was delicate, regarding us as
mothers might their babies,
summer was bursting, the sea was pierced with boats,
at night, the moon pulled itself out of the sky
on the podium a band was playing
I longed without understanding for something in the night
was left with Mr. Dodgson, trying patiently,
his hands moving as precisely as a musician's
on the black and white paper
to show me how a syllogism might be solved.

1898 (2):

At night now that it is near the end
I add up my life
sometimes troubled by doubts like serpents
that creep beneath the covers
making me recoil in horror
feeling we live in an enormous and puzzling
room
where a trial continuously takes place
and where the sentence is always
death
but this I know:
I have always loved Tuesdays
have kept in my room toys that whistle fly
or smile
marionettes to pull for the laughter of children
whose sweet faces come to me in dreams
whose soft bodies I have returned to them
in print

I feel sometimes I have not said enough
there is a list among my lists
still unfinished

But in the daylight the doubts
remove themselves like a fading smile

And I believe in life
because it is absurd.

Epilogue: Alice in New York, 1932
(the centenary of Lewis Carroll's birth)

They brought me over on a blur of continuous startling waves,
in a ship that would go backwards with a cheshire flag
and the oddity of the trip was instantly defined,
sailing under the smile of a make-believe cat
New York became interlocked cars that flew through the city
hands disentangled from bodies holding books for me to sign

what should I say
what name do I have
I am certain it is not the one they want

the Waldorf suite with its ringing ceiling
and the rounding mirrors plumping like balloons

the flashbulbs waiting waiting
for a child with long blond hair a stark face
and stockings that wind around her like a barber pole

Your hair-then it was never fair?
there is a mouth behind a camera

It was always dark—till now,

they are studying me, I am eighty, my hands are carded with age,
I have gone through a startling transformation,
they are looking to see how many rabbit holes and
playhouses enclose me,
how many chess boards I folded away

they are taking me at my words

but there is no longer any meaning in them

I am caught in a maze
not of my own making.